FAMOUS ARTISTS
MIRÓ

The author Nicholas Ross is a director of Art History Abroad Courses Limited,
and the author of several art books.

Designer	Peter Bennett
Editor	Katie Roden
Picture research	Brooks Krikler Research
Illustrator	Michaela Stewart

First edition for the United States, Canada, and the Philippines
published 1995 by Barron's Educational Series, Inc.

Designed and produced by
Aladdin Books Ltd
28 Percy Street
London W1P 0LD

First published in
Great Britain in 1995 by
Watts Books
96 Leonard Street
London EC2A 4RH

All inquiries should be addressed to:
Barron's Educational Series, Inc.
250 Wireless Boulevard
Hauppauge, New York 11788

Library of Congress Catalog Card No.: 95-35420

International Standard Book No. 0-8120-6535-2 (hardcover)
0-8120-9427-1 (paperback)

Library of Congress Cataloging-in-Publication Data
Ross, Nicholas.
Miró / Nicholas Ross. – 1st U.S. ed.
p. cm. – (Famous artists)
Includes index.
Summary: Explores Miró's life and development as an artist, his entry into surrealism, and his
versatility in abstract expression. Includes a brief history of art.
ISBN 0-8120-6535-2 (hc). – ISBN 0-8120-9427-1 (pbk.)
1. Miró, Joan, 1893–Juvenile literature. 2. Artists–Spain–Catalonia–Biography–Juvenile literature.
[1. Miró, Joan. 1893-. 2. Artists. 3. Art appreciation.] I. Title. II. Series.
N7113.M54R67 1995
709'.2–dc20
[B]   95-35420
CIP
AC
Printed in Belgium
5678 4208 987654321

FAMOUS ARTISTS

MIRÓ

NICHOLAS ROSS

BARRON'S

CONTENTS

 To create *Burnt Picture I*, in 1973, Miró first painted the canvas with acrylic paint, then singed it, to create a random, unique effect.

INTRODUCTION

Joan Miró (1893~1983) is widely considered to be one of the most versatile masters of twentieth~century art. He is often described as a Spanish Surrealist, but even a brief glance at the following pages will reveal Miró to be many different artists in one. Miró used painting, sculpture, textiles, pottery, theater, and enormous public monuments to express his ideas, which have had a lasting influence and show him to be a truly international artist. He was enormously proud of his homeland, Catalonia in northeastern Spain, and of his hometown, Barcelona, which was also home to other artists including Pablo Picasso, Salvador Dali, and Antoni Gaudí. Miró was an exciting artist in an exciting time. The variety of his abstract vision is explained in this book, and by using the activity boxes you can explore his ideas for yourself. Below you can see how the book is organized.

Illustration of the artist's home or environment

The story of the artist's life

About the artist's work at the time

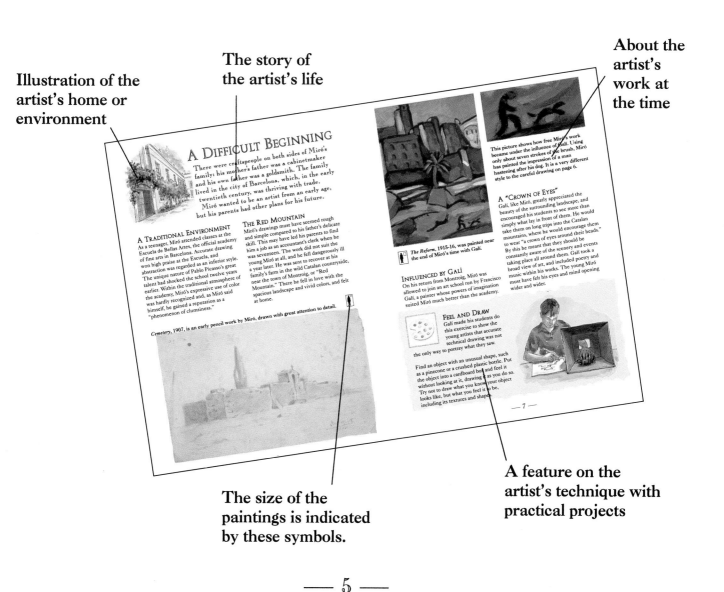

The size of the paintings is indicated by these symbols.

A feature on the artist's technique with practical projects

A DIFFICULT BEGINNING

There were craftspeople on both sides of Miró's family: his mother's father was a cabinetmaker and his own father was a goldsmith. The family lived in the city of Barcelona, which, in the early twentieth century, was thriving with trade.

Miró wanted to be an artist from an early age, but his parents had other plans for his future.

A TRADITIONAL ENVIRONMENT

As a teenager, Miró attended classes at the Escuela de Bellas Artes, the official academy of fine arts in Barcelona. Accurate drawing won high praise at the Escuela, and abstraction was regarded as an inferior style. The unique nature of Pablo Picasso's great talent had shocked the school twelve years earlier. Within the traditional atmosphere of the academy, Miró's expressive use of color was hardly recognized and, as Miró said himself, he gained a reputation as a "phenomenon of clumsiness."

THE RED MOUNTAIN

Miró's drawings must have seemed rough and simple compared to his father's delicate skill. This may have led his parents to find him a job as an accountant's clerk when he was seventeen. The work did not suit the young Miró at all, and he fell dangerously ill a year later. He was sent to recover at his family's farm in the wild Catalan countryside, near the town of Montroig, or "Red Mountain." There he fell in love with the spacious landscape and vivid colors, and felt at home.

Cemetery, 1907, is an early pencil work by Miró, drawn with great attention to detail.

This picture shows how free Miró's work became under the influence of Galí. Using only about seven strokes of the brush, Miró has painted the impression of a man hastening after his dog. It is a very different style to the careful drawing on page 6.

 *The Reform*, 1915-16, was painted near the end of Miró's time with Galí.

INFLUENCED BY GALÍ

On his return from Montroig, Miró was allowed to join an art school run by Francisco Galí, a painter whose powers of imagination suited Miró much better than the academy.

A "CROWN OF EYES"

Galí, like Miró, greatly appreciated the beauty of the surrounding landscape, and encouraged his students to see more than simply what lay in front of them. He would take them on long trips into the Catalan mountains, where he would encourage them to wear "a crown of eyes around their heads." By this he meant that they should be constantly aware of the scenery and events taking place all around them. Galí took a broad view of art, and included poetry and music within his works. The young Miró must have felt his eyes and mind opening wider and wider.

FEEL AND DRAW

Galí made his students do this exercise to show the young artists that accurate technical drawing was not the only way to portray what they saw.

Find an object with an unusual shape, such as a pinecone or a crushed plastic bottle. Put the object into a cardboard box and feel it without looking at it, drawing it as you do so. Try not to draw what you know your object looks like, but what you feel it to be, including its textures and shapes.

CATALAN PRIDE

Although Miró became internationally recognized, he always remained Catalan and proud of his province in northeastern Spain. After leaving Francisco Galí's school in 1915, Miró and some other artists joined together to develop a modern, recognizably Catalan style of painting.

A GROWING NATIONALISM

In 1915 Miró became a member of the Cercle Artistic de Sant Lluc, founded in 1893. With his lifelong friends Joan Prats, Josep Llorens Artigas, J. F. Ràfols, and E. C. Ricart, Miró painted at Vilanova (above), 31 miles (50 km) from Barcelona, and met artists like Antonio Gaudí. Of all the artists and architects of the period, Gaudí best showed Catalan pride – he never left Barcelona. His imaginative buildings were modern and unique, with no reference to the past. Such nationalism coincided with the founding in 1901 of the Conservative Nationalist Party, and a decree by the government in 1913 that Catalonia should have more independence within Spain.

The First World War was raging in Europe. This prevented easy travel to Paris, which was a center of avant-garde thinking. But culture from Paris did reach Spain, thanks to the art dealer Josep Dalmau. He put together exhibitions of artists such as Matisse, Rédon, and Cézanne, which introduced Miró and his friends to the ideas of cubism and fauvism.

Siurana, the Village, 1917, is made of blocks of color, in a Fauvist style.

 Portrait of V. Nubiola, painted in 1917, shows some signs of cubism.

The eucalyptus tree is common in Catalonia. Here its shape is simplified so that it represents the place rather than one tree. The sky has many different cloud formations, to show different types of sky over the year.

Vegetable Garden with Donkey, 1918, shows Miró's use of a variety of styles.

THE CATALAN CHARACTER

Miró and his friends aimed for the "mystical dimension of the Catalan temperament." They wanted to paint in such a way as to include the "lived experience" of a place – both its history and the artist's memory of a scene. Common features of the Catalan landscape appeared regularly in these pictures. Carob and eucalyptus trees, snails, and snakes were used as symbols to suggest the atmosphere of the local landscape rather than representing one particular object. Miró believed that there were two sides to the Catalan nature – passion and a down-to-earth approach to life.

In his paintings of this period, the passion was represented by strong, flat colors and the realistic aspect by fine, detailed line. This mingling of styles symbolized the two sides of the Catalan character to Miró, although it seemed strange to many people.

PAINT IN COLOR ALONE

The Fauvists, whose style greatly influenced Miró, used color to make shapes, rather than "filling in" a drawn outline.

Paint the buildings around your home or school without using one line to enclose any shape. Build your picture with bold colors. Darker colors are better for the foreground and lighter ones give a sense of depth. Red "jumps out" at you, while blue "sinks" into the depths of the picture. Be bold and imaginative with your choice of colors. For example, we know that a road is made of black tar, but in some sorts of light it may look purple or blue.

A Taste of Paris

Early in 1918, the art dealer Dalmau put on Miró's first solo exhibition, in Barcelona. Miró saw this as the end of one period of his life and the beginning of another. Leaving the Cercle Artistic de Sant Lluc, he left Barcelona as he strove to become ever more modern in his approach.

A Dramatic Impression

By 1919 the war in Europe was over, and Miró made his first journey to Paris (above) in March. The many avant-garde ideas in Paris and the enormous range of great artists in the Louvre museum may have overwhelmed Miró, and he returned home without painting a single canvas. He returned to Montroig, and began to search for a new reality in his painting. He painted every detail of his subjects, including aspects that could not be seen but were known to be there. For example, in his picture of Montroig, he included details of the drainage system. Similarly, Miró might have painted a bright sun to represent the climate, but he would not have always painted the shadows it cast, because they would hide objects.

Village and Church of Montroig, of 1919, includes many aspects of Miró's subject, including the town sewers.

The Farm, 1922, is an inventory of every detail of a small farm.

This style of painting was completely new, and went against many popular ideas of the time, such as impressionism. Whereas other artists tried to focus on just one aspect of their surroundings, Miró tried to include everything that he knew to be real. There was no hint of the styles or techniques of the past in Miró's new work.

The Farmer's Wife was painted in both Spain and Paris in 1922-23.

This painting shows the influence of Picasso and cubism on some of Miró's early works. The woman is shown from several angles at once. Some of her features, such as her work-roughened hands and feet, are emphasized.

BACK TO FRANCE

Toward the end of 1920, Miró moved back to Paris and found some studio space at 45 rue Blomet. He passed the winters in Paris and the summers in his beloved Catalonia. Throughout this time, he lived in a state of near poverty, eating only one proper lunch a week. In 1921 the faithful art dealer Dalmau organized a solo exhibition, at which Miró was unable to sell one picture. Yet he did not lose hope, and continued to paint. In 1922 he painted *The Farm* (far left), which showed his recent ideas and technique very clearly. This was an accurate picture of Miró's family farm. It contained many of the elements of his Catalan style, such as the eucalyptus tree. Miró was so fond of the picture, and so determined to finish it, that he took it with him when he traveled. In 1925 *The Farm* was sold to the famous American writer Ernest Hemingway.

COMPLETE REALITY

Miró used the technique of "complete reality" in many of his paintings during this period. He chose to show the less pleasant aspects of a scene, such as the sewers underneath a picturesque Catalan landscape, as well as the beautiful ones, to give his pictures greater depth.

If you draw your room, you probably draw only what you can see when you look around you – the furniture, windows, doors, and carpets, for example. But does that truly represent everything that you know about your room? What about the shoes under the bed, the stuffing in your pillow, or your clothes in the drawer? They are also a part of your room. There are many other parts that you know to be there: the plasterboard behind the paint, the electric wires in the wall, the pipes in the ceiling, or the floorboards under the carpet. All these things make up the reality of your room. Try drawing or painting your room including all these invisible aspects as well as the visible ones. Your finished drawing may not look as realistic as an ordinary drawing, but it will show everything that is really there.

SURREALISM

Miró met the poet Tristan Tzara, a celebrity of the Dada movement, in 1920, but it was not until 1923 that his art started to move toward dadaism and surrealism. At this time Miró met many contemporary poets. He began to form a group of artistic friends who were based around his studio at rue Blomet.

A NEW VIEWPOINT

The Dada movement fought against reason, logic, and traditional methods of artistic expression. It included theater, poetry, political theory, and art, and it emerged from the social and physical destruction caused by the First World War. It had no respect for the ways of thinking of the past. The artists of the Dada movement aimed for imaginative and unique ways of expressing themselves. Their style had no traditional structure or meanings, and so was independent.

A TRUE SURREALIST

In 1924 the poet André Breton published a *Surrealist Manifesto*, in which he wrote, "I believe in the future resolution of these two states...which are dreams and reality, a sort of absolute reality, or surreality." Surrealism, like the Dada movement, was made up largely of poets and writers who wanted to break away from traditional art forms. Many Surrealists began to write in a way similar to Miró's style of painting. Breton later declared: "Miró is the most surreal of us all."

Composition, 1927, shows the influence of surrealism on Miró, in his linking of random images.

GROWING RECOGNITION

In 1925 an exhibition called *La Révolution Surréaliste* (The Surrealist Revolution) was staged at the Galerie Pierre in Paris, at which the work of both poets and painters was shown. *Harlequin's Carnival* (see page 13) was shown with two other pictures by Miró and, at the age of thirty two, he was universally acclaimed. A *Galerie Surréaliste* (Surrealist Gallery) was opened in the following year, to show the work of famous Surrealists including Miró, Man Ray, Max Ernst, André Masson, and Marcel Duchamp.

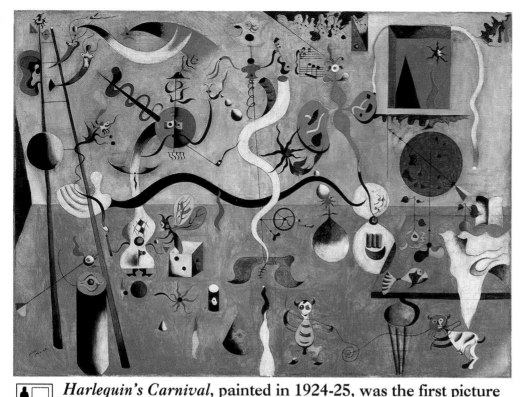

Eyes form an important symbol within Miró's work of this period. They never express any emotion, but are usually included as symbols. The eye here shows that this cylinder represents a person. One shade of blue links many of the images.

 *Harlequin's Carnival*, painted in 1924-25, was the first picture by Miró to receive popular acclaim.

HARLEQUIN'S CARNIVAL

Harlequin's Carnival was the last, most surreal picture of this period in Miró's career. The Harlequin looks out with a half-red, half-blue face, smoking a pipe, and with the familiar diamond pattern on his chest. Nearby is a guitarist, and two cats play in the foreground.

There is no specific meaning to this picture, and no traditional rules of painting are observed. It is a random choice of images in an illogical arrangement. Miró made no attempt to explore the workings of the mind. He simply tried to paint the bizarre yet creative nature of our dreams.

PAINTING WITH SYMBOLS

Miró used symbols rather than accurate drawings in *Harlequin's Carnival*. Sometimes symbols can be more effective than realistic pictures, as they show the elements of a scene that are most important or moving to the artist. Try using symbols to represent an aspect of your everyday life.

Take a familiar theme or situation, such as your classroom. Imagine all the different characters among the pupils and teachers. Try to represent all this by using symbols or caricatures rather than realistic drawings, so that someone else (even a person you do not know) could understand some aspects of your school life. Important people, such as your best friends or your teachers, might be larger. Color might suggest mood – for example, red is often used to show anger, whereas blue can represent calmness or sadness. You could use symbols to show different people according to their interests or hobbies. Instead of drawing a person, you could draw a giant football, a big bag of sweets, the musical instrument that the person plays, or anything else that reminds you of that person.

INSPIRED BY OTHERS

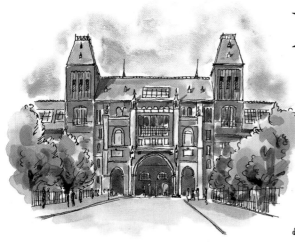

In 1928 Miró visited the Netherlands. He was impressed by the seventeenth-century paintings in the museums (left), particularly those of Vermeer. He was fascinated by the way in which small, ordinary objects like a jug or a knife were treated with the same attention to detail as the main subject.

TENSIONS WITHIN SURREALISM

The Surrealist movement had grown stronger after 1925, but cracks had begun to appear within it. Political arguments, and the risk of offending André Breton, drove Miró away from the group. He was treated with growing suspicion for holding his own views, which he tended to keep to himself.

When Miró and the artist Max Ernst created a stage set for the opera *Romeo and Juliet* in 1926, Breton staged a demonstration outside the theater. He accused Miró and Ernst of indulging in middle-class, meaningless creative activities that completely contradicted the revolutionary spirit of the surrealist movement.

ART ON MANY LEVELS

Miró went to the Netherlands, where his style began to change once again. He aimed to combine the accurate detail used by the Dutch master painters with his own abstract style. This seems to be a contradiction: how can a detail be recognized as a detail once it is abstracted? The letter in the picture on the left is not a detailed drawing but an abstract image representing a letter. However, the letter is a detailed part of an existing picture, *Mrs. Mills Reading a Letter*, painted by George Engleheart in 1750. Miró's portrayal of the letter is therefore recognizable as an abstraction of another artist's detail.

 A Portrait of Mrs. Mills in 1750, painted in 1929, was based on a painting by Engleheart.

Miró has summarized the character of the spaniel in Sorgh's painting in a very amusing way. In the original picture, the dog is shown to be pampered and rather stupid. Miró has shown the dog smoking a pipe and staring blankly out at the viewer.

Dutch Interior I, 1928, was based on *The Lute Player* by H. M. Sorgh.

INFLUENCED BY THE MASTERS

Miró's *Dutch Interior I* was also an abstracted version of an existing painting. Its composition and features were taken directly from a painting by the Dutch master Hendrick Martensz Sorgh (1610-70), called *The Lute Player*. Miró painted in such a way for a short time, but he quickly moved on to even greater degrees of abstraction.

MARRIAGE AND FAMILY

For two years Miró had lived on the rue Tourlaque in Paris. In 1929, he married Pilar Juncosa, who gave birth to a daughter, Maria Dolores, in 1931. The family continued to live in Paris, but they had to move to a cheaper area of the city because a fall in the demand for modern art had left Miró short of money. Every summer the family went to Catalonia or to Palma on Majorca, where Miró's mother owned some property.

ABSTRACT A PICTURE

Find a famous picture by a master painter, such as Botticelli's *The Birth of Venus* or da Vinci's *Mona Lisa*.

Make your own version by replacing the main features of the picture with symbols or exaggerated details. Decide which elements of the original picture are the most important or interesting to you, and make them prominent in your version with exaggeration or bold colors. For example, you may find the background to the *Mona Lisa* fascinating, so emphasize some of the features within it – there are craggy mountains, wide rivers, and a bridge. Or you could emphasize Venus's flowing red hair, the angels flying beside her or the flowers being carried in the wind.

A similar technique of redrawing well-known works of art or people is often used in satirical cartoons in newspapers. A cartoonist may abstract certain features of a public figure, for example, by making them enormously large. The cartoon is funny because the viewer recognizes the exaggerated features as a representation of someone well known. Try making your own cartoons of well-known people.

War in Art and Life

Miró now began to experiment with the traditional medium in which artists had worked for centuries — paint and canvas. This was the beginning of a period in which he "assassinated painting" by using colored paper, cloth, or any found objects ("objets trouvés," left) to make pictures.

The Spanish Civil War

In 1933 Miró returned to Barcelona with his family, to spend some time working on his paintings, but his stay was cut short. Spanish politics were forced to dangerous extremes in the 1930s, with the growth of the opposing Fascist and Communist movements. In July 1936, a grueling civil war broke out in Spain, between the Fascists under General Franco and the Communist-led Republicans. Miró was a Republican, like many people in Catalonia, and the war forced him and his family to leave Barcelona for Paris again.

The End of the Dream

The main image of *The Reaper* is a peasant from Catalonia, a subject that had been featured in many of Miró's previous paintings. However, this picture did not represent a harmonious or pleasant view of Catalonia, but demonstrated Miró's anger at the war. Miró showed the peasant shouting violently, as if voicing his rage about the war and his determination not to be down-trodden. Despite the picture's vast size, however, it mysteriously disappeared during the journey back from the exhibition.

Years of Hardship

Economic depression had damaged the art market in Europe, leading to several years of poverty for Miró and his family. This difficult life and the cruel nature of the war in Spain affected Miró greatly. What he described as his "wild paintings" were produced during this period. These pictures featured large, monstrous beings formed by harsh lines and ugly colors. In the Paris International Exhibition of 1937, one such painting, a mural called *The Reaper*, was displayed next to Picasso's famous criticism of war, *Guernica*. It covered a whole wall of the large Spanish Pavilion.

Painting Based on a Collage, 1933.

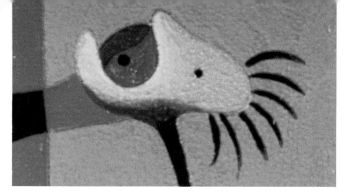

Throughout Miró's paintings, his lines were usually curvy and gentle. In the Civil War period there appeared a new sense of horror, which caused him to paint shocking images such as this screaming woman.

Flame in Space and Female Nude, 1932, is one of Miró's "wild paintings."

"AIDEZ L'ESPAGNE"
Miró became further involved with contemporary events when he designed a powerful poster entitled *Aidez l'Espagne* ("Help Spain"). The poster (see page 20) was sold across Europe for one French franc per copy, to raise money for the Spanish Republican movement. Miró said at the time: "In the present struggle I can see, on the one hand, the Fascists as an antagonistic force, on the other, the people." This sympathy with the Spanish people is clear in all his major works painted during the Spanish Civil War.

REPRESENTING THE PEOPLE
In his works of this period, Miró captured the moods of all the people of Spain. His paintings were reflections of the hopes, fears, and dreams of everybody in the country; they were not intended to deliver his personal intellectual or political message.

FLAT COLORS
Make a simple design of a portrait or a street scene, then paint the picture using flat areas of plain color.

Choose strong colors such as Chinese red, cobalt blue, or chrome yellow, and lay them down as areas of pure color. Remember that different colors and types of paint have different textures and impact. Allow the paper, canvas, or board underneath your color to show through in places.

CONSTELLATIONS

In 1939 the rise of the German Nazi Party threatened another major war in Europe. Miró moved his family from Paris to Varengeville, Normandy, in the following year. The stormy skies and dramatic beaches of Normandy restored his faith in nature and inspired yet another change in his artistic style.

THE FLIGHT FROM THE NAZIS

Miró later said of his time in Normandy: "I felt a deep desire to escape. I deliberately shut up my mind. The night, music, and the stars began to play an increasingly important role in my pictures." At this time he began a series of pictures known as the *Constellations*. However, in the middle of his work he was forced to escape the advancing German army by moving his family to Barcelona.

Painting with an Art Nouveau Frame, **1943.**

To create *Woman Encircled by the Flight of a Bird* in 1941, Miró drew a random line, then filled it in with color.

The family raced to Paris, where they boarded the last train to leave for Barcelona before the Nazis overran the city. Miró could not stay in Barcelona. His *Aidez l'Espagne* poster had displayed his Republican feelings too strongly, and the new Fascist government refused to accept him. He moved his family to Palma, on Majorca (top left).

This simple detail shows a woman looking out at the viewer, with an anguished face. The figures at the bottom seem more aggressive; perhaps they represent the brutality of war, whereas the woman symbolizes an innocent victim.

Barcelona Suite IV, 1944. This is one of 50 lithographs that made Miró famous.

A SURPRISING HARMONY

The *Constellations* were finished in Palma, and showed none of the harsh lines of Miró's "wild paintings." The positions of the figures were not aggressive, and the compositions were evenly spread with balanced colors. Miró composed the *Constellations* by first drawing a random line on the paper. He then allowed himself to find shapes and figures within the line, which he filled in and decorated with paint. By the time Miró and his family were able to move back to Barcelona, in 1942, he was using a unique visual language.

BACK TO A HARSHER VISION

Miró soon returned to a stronger style, however. The *Barcelona Suite* contained fifty harsh lithographs which revealed his feelings of anguish about the Second World War.

DRAWING BY CHANCE

This technique of random, imaginative drawing was used by Miró in his *Constellations* series. He gave all these works descriptive, poetic names, such as *The Nightingale's Song at Midnight and the Morning Rain*, or *People in the Night Guided by the Phosphorescent Tracks of Snails*.

Using a black pen, close your eyes and make a bold but random squiggle on a plain piece of paper. Now look at your line and allow your imagination to see shapes and pictures within the squiggle. Fill in or add to the shapes, using different colors and adding features such as faces or hair, but be careful not to hide the original black line completely. When you have finished, look carefully at all the images you have created on your paper. Try to give the picture a title that accurately describes and links all the elements within it, like the long titles that Miró gave to his *Constellations* pictures.

GRAPHICS AND CERAMICS

Only Picasso came close to Miró in the range of materials and references he used to make pictures, sculptures, ceramic designs, stage sets, and prints. Miró enjoyed working as a team with other craftspeople; for example, he combined printers' technical knowledge with his imagination to explore a huge range of surfaces and effects.

BEGINNINGS IN PRINT

Miró's earliest prints had been made to illustrate a book of poems called *L'Arbre des Voyageurs* by the poet Tristan Tzara in 1929. In the following years he had created designs for many of the greatest poets in Europe. When, in 1937, Miró had made his powerful print *Aidez l'Espagne*, he had realized the power and popular appeal of print. He liked the fact that affordable prints could convey art throughout society, when such opportunities had previously been available only to the rich.

Aidez l'Espagne, 1937. With simple power, Miró's picture expresses the fears and determination of the Catalan people.

THE EFFECTS OF FAME

The *Barcelona Suite* spread the name of Miró around the world after 1942. His new interest in prints meant that he could design even more spontaneous compositions. He sent his ideas to a team of print makers to publish, and so could travel and create widely available art at the same time, increasing his status as a truly international artist.

One of Miró's lithographs for Tristan Tzara's *Parler Seul*, of 1948-50.

20 —

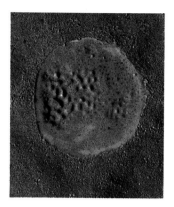

When working with ceramics, an artist can use differing textures, such as this thick paint. This is one of 200 plaques that Miró made with Artigas in the late 1940s.

CERAMICS AND POTTERY

The ceramicist Josep Llorens Artigas and Miró shared a friendship that went back as far as 1915. During the Second World War they met again. At Artigas's ceramic studio, Miró noticed a pile of imperfect pottery that lay broken by the kiln. He was immediately interested by the lack of control in the heat of a kiln, and by the infinite variety of chance effects in the firing process. In the 1950s Artigas built new kilns near Miró's studio, outside Barcelona. To Miró, ceramics were a mixture of sculpture and painting, allowing him to use color and work in three dimensions at the same time.

Estela de doble care, 1956.

RESPOND TO SOUND

Miró's many illustrations for poetry used this technique to echo the variety of feelings and moods within each poem, so creating a piece of art that was perfectly in tune with the meaning of the words.

Find a piece of music that contains many different moods. For example, a good piece to choose is Ravel's *Bolero*. It is the same tune played continuously but by a series of individual instruments, to create a variety of sounds and atmospheres. While listening to the music, draw on a large piece of paper a line or colors that best represent the sounds you are hearing. Think of the pitch and rhythm of the sounds, and the feelings that the music stirs in you. Use flowing or sharp lines and different colors. If the music is lively and snappy, you could draw zig-zag lines or dots. Red or orange might be good colors to choose. If it is sad and slow, try flowing, smooth lines and dark colors. Now try this technique with a poem. Ask a friend to read it out loud and "draw the poem" as he or she does so. As with the music, choose shapes and colors that correspond to the moods of the poem. Perhaps you could make a book of illustrated poems with your friends.

INTERNATIONAL FAME

For the first two years after the war, Miró remained relatively unknown while he continued to experiment with a variety of styles. In 1947 he traveled to New York (left). Although he was stimulated by his experience of the United States and was received there enthusiastically, his painting was not greatly influenced by the country.

A WARM WELCOME

Miró's art was already known in New York, where there had been a retrospective of his work in 1941. When he arrived he was eagerly greeted by his old Surrealist friends who had settled there, such as Marcel Duchamp. The art world also appreciated Miró's work greatly, because he looked for new forms of expression that had no reference to traditional art forms. Almost immediately he was commissioned to paint a mural, 99 feet (30 m) square, in the dining room of the Terrace Plaza Hotel in Cincinnati.

A VARIETY OF MEDIA

By this time, Miró's paintings comprised two categories. He described the first as his "slow paintings," in which he took care to make his lines perfect, as in his earlier works such as *The Farm*. The second type of painting was completely spontaneous. In both types he paid great attention to the painting's background. This could be made of almost anything: burlap, board, brown wrapping paper, or canvas, under which might be laid wire or plaster that stuck through the painted surface. One of Miró's favorite devices was to poke string through from the back and knot it at the front of the picture. There was almost no material or medium that Miró did not explore – he even used black currant jam to create a picture on one occasion.

Miró did not want to control this vast range of materials and styles, to make them a permanent feature of his work, or to perfect the use of them. He simply explored their potential as ways of creating new, exciting forms of art that could be groundbreaking and accessible at the same time.

 Woman and Bird in the Night, 1945, shows Miró's spontaneous style.

To create the painting's mottled effect, Miró has scrubbed down the canvas as far as the weave. Some areas are more intense. The light and dark patches around this star emphasize it within the picture.

 *The Smile of Flaming Wings*, 1953, shows the refined lines and careful coloring of Miró's "slow paintings."

A RETURN TO FRANCE

In 1947 Miró returned to Paris, where he received a warm welcome after his long absence. The Galerie Maeght held a retrospective of his work, which increased his position as an international artist.

Miró then returned to Barcelona, where he entered into a period of enormous artistic output. He produced 55 paintings and more than 150 finished drawings between 1949 and 1950, as well as numerous uncompleted sketches and designs.

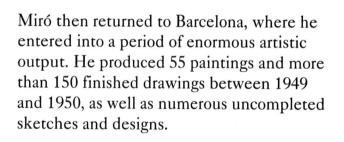

CREATE ART ON A STRANGE SURFACE

Miró experimented with a wide range of backgrounds to his paintings.

Explore the effects of drawing or making a collage on an unusual background. Use anything you can find: a supermarket bag, a stone, an old record, a tile (shown here), or a piece of textured wallpaper, for example. Each background will affect the look and atmosphere of your picture, and may influence the subject you choose.

SCULPTURE

Miró saw sculpture as a way of taking art to all people, saying: "I want to try . . . to go beyond easel painting . . . and get nearer to the masses of whom I have never ceased to be aware." Other people, such as his friend Joan Prats, saw sculpture as a wide field within which Miró could work. Prats observed: "When I pick up a stone, it's a stone. When Miró picks up a stone, it's a Miró."

PUBLIC MONUMENTS

The use of "objets trouvés" (found objects) in Miró's art of the 1930s had more to do with the development of surrealism than with pure sculpture. In the 1950s Miró again returned to sculpture, but now based it on chance shapes and images. Miró's most famous sculptures date from the 1960s. In 1968 an enormous exhibition took place in Barcelona, where every aspect of Miró's work was displayed. The city also commissioned three monumental sculptures from Miró.

These included a 197-foot (60-m) high sculpture on the hills overlooking the city, a pavement design to extend the length of the city's main road, the Ramblas, and a mural at the Barcelona airport. Miró was inspired by the simplicity of traditional Catalan sculpture. Yet his use of "objets trouvés" showed how he saw all materials and objects as useful.

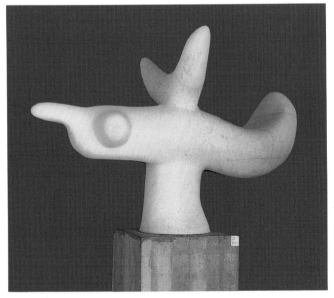

 Sun Bird, 1968 was first cast in bronze, and later carved in marble.

Personage and Bird, 1968. The rough patina was added by José Parellada.

Everlasting Art

Once his arrangements were assembled, Miró would have them cast in bronze. The structures would thus become fixed and long lasting, and could be reproduced easily if necessary. Miró enjoyed the new textures that other materials brought, as well as the "chance" occurrences of casting. Once set, the bronze could be decorated with a patina (for example a film of copper) or changed by weather. In some cases, Miró painted the bronze.

Mixing Media

Miró was interested in what happened when one art medium crossed into another. He enjoyed the different effects created by placing the same sculpture inside a room and outside.

Personage with Three Legs, 1967. **Miró liked the image of an agricultural fork, which was a very common tool in rural Catalonia.**

Capturing Space

Miró saw sculpture as affecting the space it used, and changing the space it sat within. The fork rising above the sculpture on the left prongs the sky above; without it this piece would be quite different and would not dominate the space so strongly. In 1964 Miró was given the chance to explore sculpture within space, when the Maeght Foundation was established on the hillside of Saint Paul de Vence in Provence. Among trees, surrounded by water, and set against the sea to one side and hills inland, Miró made sculptures of which the object itself was only a small part; it was the space and the natural landscape around the works that gave them their beauty and power. Each sculpture was placed carefully within the grounds of the Foundation so that it complemented the other works and the walls of the building as well as sat comfortably and dramatically within the beautiful natural surroundings.

Sculpting in Space

In his sculpture, Miró was always very keen to experiment with the space occupied by each piece, and how its appearance and meaning were affected by placing it in different surroundings and next to a variety of objects.

Find various objects with different textures and interesting shapes, and arrange them to make an unusual shape or figure. Remember that certain objects may remind you of something that could give your sculpture symbolic meaning; for example, Miró saw the shape of an agricultural fork as a symbol for the lives and feelings of the peasants of Catalonia. Like Miró, you could color with paint or dye to make the most important parts of the sculpture stand out. Set your work in various indoor settings, then place it outside against a building, the sky, or some trees, and see if your impression of your sculpture changes. Almost all sculpture is made to stand on the ground. Why not be different and hang it from some rafters or the branch of a tree?

ACCLAIM AT HOME

In 1956 Miró saw the fulfillment of a dream he had held for over twenty years. His good friend, the architect José Luis Sert, designed a large studio for him outside Palma. In 1959 he received an award from President Eisenhower. After 1959 Miró's paintings became almost completely abstract. In the late 1960s the idea of a Miró Foundation was explored by Joan Prats, but Prats died in 1970. Sert later built the Foundation. Miró became more and more recognized by the world.

ENORMOUS CREATIVITY

For much of the 1950s Miró had been engaged in sculptural and ceramic projects, but in 1959 he began to paint with renewed vigor, producing more than 100 canvases in a year. He expanded his visual language to mix together different techniques and symbols that he had previously used only separately. For example, the types of fine line that he had used in the *Constellations* series were set against pure color backgrounds, where previously they had been painted on mottled effects. The bold, almost violent lines of his gloomy prewar period were now mixed with delicate images of stars against bright colors. Miró used blemishes, imperfections, or manufacturers' trademarks on a canvas as a starting point for inspiration, or threw pots of paint onto the surface, in a way similar to Jackson Pollock. This allowed him to explore even further the artistic possibilities of chance effects.

In his 1975 works for La Défense in Paris, Miró used abstract forms to show emotions.

 For Emili Fernández Miró, 1963. Miró used both bright colors and fine lines.

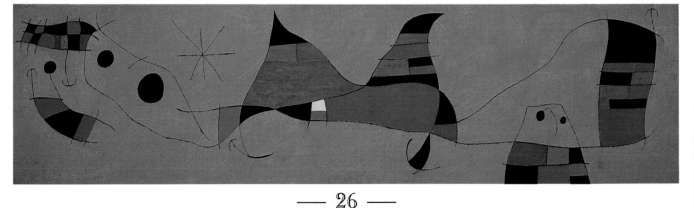

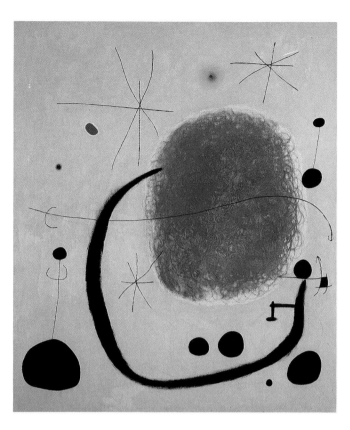

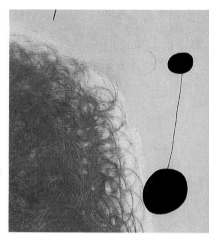

This simple picture, from one of Miró's most productive periods, explores the enormous range of textures available within different colors. Thick, bold lines, thin fine lines, blue, viscous red, and pure yellow are all combined within it.

In *The Gold of the Azure*, 1967, Miró creates variety but maintains order.

DEMOCRATIC ART

It would be a mistake to look deeply for lots of meaning or messages in the work of Miró. He wanted people to be able to interpret his work in their own way. Miró's paintings, tapestries, and sculptures were for everyone – nobody needed a particular intellectual background to enjoy his work, just eyes with which to see – making it a truly democratic art. This does not mean that Miró was not a skilled artist; it took him decades to make his images so clear, unique, and immediate.

RECOGNITION IN SPAIN

For Miró, 1968 was a special year. The vast retrospective exhibition and public monuments in Barcelona celebrated his achievements for the first time in his own country, as Franco's Fascist regime was coming to an end. Having been acclaimed worldwide, Miró had come home to stay.

EXPRESSIVE ART

In many of his later works, like the sculptures for La Défense (see page 26), Miró represented the feelings and expressions of his subjects by using abstract, exaggerated features and gestures, such as large eyes and sweeping body movements.

Practice this form of exaggerated representation by looking at pictures of sports figures in the newspaper. Trace their faces or dramatic movements, then exaggerate your drawn line so that its shape expresses the person's emotions, such as the joy of a winning athlete. Then draw some imaginary people in this way, emphasising features that reveal their personality. A greedy person might have a large mouth and hands, while a sad person could be shown with big, tearful eyes and a stooping body. Cartoonists use this sort of distortion all the time, to show extreme emotions like surprise, anger, happiness, and sorrow. Try to take this further to express more subtle ideas like energy, patience, or effort.

THEATER AND TAPESTRY

Throughout his life, Miró had worked in many fields of art — sculpture, ceramics, and printing as well as painting. By nature he was a modest man who liked teamwork. He therefore greatly enjoyed making set and costume designs for plays and ballets, which closely complemented the script or music. He also worked as part of a team when making his monumental tapestries, which were always carefully designed to match and enhance the surrounding architecture.

BEGINNINGS IN THEATER

Miró had first become involved with the theater as early as 1926, when he had designed and painted the set for the Russian Ballet's production of *Romeo and Juliet,* with the Surrealist painter Max Ernst. Unfortunately, no records of these designs have survived.

THE BIRD OF LIGHT

A few years later, a dance choreographer, Léonide Massine, saw some of Miró's brightly colored abstract paintings. Massine realized that Miró would be able to express the imaginative world of children in a set for his ballet *Jeux d'Enfants* ("Children's Games"). Miró designed the set, toys, and costumes for the ballet, which was first performed in 1932. For Miró, the opportunity to work on such a large scale was very exciting; he saw the ballet as a huge picture with moving parts. In 1978 the Claca theater company asked Miró to design costumes for *Mori el Merma,* about a brutal dictator named Ubu Roi. The theme of bullying leaders reminded Miró of Franco, and he designed powerful, grotesque, and shocking costumes for the production. Miró's last work in the theater, in 1981, was almost autobiographical. He designed the costumes for a dance called *Miró, l'Uccello Luce* ("Miró, the Bird of Light"). The music, by Sylvano Bussotti, and the script, by Jacques Dupin, described the three main stages in Miró's career: his search for an artistic identity; his imaginative "dream world" period; and his final discovery of a versatile, unique artistic language.

Miró continued to create new works throughout the final years of his life.

In common with his paintings of this period, Miró continued to use strong, pure colors and powerful lines. In this tapestry, a sense of depth has been created by stitching string and cord onto the canvas and adding paint and thread.

Sobreteixim VI, 1972, is paint, rope, and wool on a jute mat.

WEAVING HIS ART

Miró's interest in tapestry came from the idea of three-dimensional pictures. In the early 1970s he would thread wool and other materials through loosely woven backgrounds like jute or sackcloth. Various "objets trouvés" could then be stitched or tied to the picture.

Blemishes and marks on the cloth were included in Miró's tapestries, and he sometimes burnt the work, and then stamped out the flames to see what patterns were left. In the last decade of his life, Miró designed some huge, shaggy tapestries whose imaginative, bold colors and lines recall his later paintings.

MAKING TAPESTRY

Like Miró, you can use burlap, netting, or any other material with holes as a background.

Thread colored string, cotton, or strips of old material through the background. You can copy the stitches shown here or make up your own effects. Try to build up blocks of color and differing textures, and stitch over the top of these with embroidery thread. Do not attempt to burn your picture.

CHRONOLOGY OF MIRÓ'S LIFE

1893 April 20: Born in Barcelona, Spain.

1907 Attends the Escuela de Bellas Artes.

1911 Works as an accountant; falls ill.

1912-15 Attends Francisco Galí's school.

1918 First solo show, at Galerías Dalmau in Barcelona.

1919 Visits Paris.

1921 Solo show in Paris.

1921-25 Meets many artists and thinkers.

1925 Highly successful show in Paris.

1926 Galerie Surrealiste opens in Paris.

1926 Designs set for *Romeo and Juliet*.

1928 First visit to the Netherlands.

1929 Marries Pilar Juncosa.

1932 *Jeux d'Enfants* first performed.

1933-36 Family settles in Barcelona.

1937 Spanish Civil War begins; Miró's family flees Spain.

1939 Outbreak of Second World War.

1940 Family settles in Majorca.

1941 Large-scale retrospective in New York.

1944 Starts ceramic work with Artigas.

1947 First visit to New York.

1947-54 Achieves worldwide status.

1955-58 Ceramics at UNESCO building, Paris.

1956 Settles in studio at Palma.

1960-68 A period of high artistic productivity.

1964 Maeght Foundation opens, with sculptures by Miró.

1968 Exhibition in Barcelona.

1972 Creation of Joan Miró Foundation.

1978 *Mori el Merma* performed.

1981 *L'Uccello Luce* performed in Venice.

1983 December 25: Miró dies.

A BRIEF HISTORY OF ART

The world's earliest works of art are figurines dating from 30,000 B.C. Cave art developed from 16,000 B.C. In the Classical Age (500-400 B.C.) sculpture flourished in Ancient Greece.

The Renaissance period began in Italy in the 1300s and reached its height in the sixteenth century. Famous Italian artists include Giotto (ca. 1266-1337), Leonardo da Vinci (1452-1519), Michelangelo Buonarroti (1475-1564), and Titian (ca. 1487-1576).

In Europe during the fifteenth and sixteenth centuries, Hieronymus Bosch (active 1480-1516), Albrecht Dürer (1471-1528), Pieter Brueghel the Elder (1525-69), and El Greco (1541-1614) produced great art. Artists of the Baroque period include Peter Paul Rubens (1577-1640) and Rembrandt van Rijn (1606-69).

During the Romantic movement, English artists J. M. W. Turner (1775-1851) and John Constable (1776-1837) produced wonderful landscapes. Francisco Goya (1746-1828) was a great Spanish portrait artist.

Impressionism began in France in the 1870s. Artists include Claude Monet (1840-1926), Camille Pissarro (1830-1903), and Edgar Degas (1834-1917). Post-Impressionists include Paul Cézanne (1839-1906), Paul Gauguin (1848-1903), and Vincent Van Gogh (1853-90).

The twentieth century has seen many movements in art. Georges Braque (1882-1963) painted in the Cubist tradition, Salvador Dali (1904-89) in the Surrealist. Pablo Picasso (1881-1973) was a prolific Spanish painter. More recently Jackson Pollock (1912-56) and David Hockney (1937-) have achieved fame.

Museums and Galleries

The following museums and galleries have examples of Miró's work:

England:
Tate Gallery, London

France:
Alexander Calder Collection, Sache
Musée du Louvre, Paris
Galerie Maeght, Paris
Musée Nationale d'Art Moderne, Paris

Germany:
Folkwang Museum Collection, Essen
Wallraf-Richartz Museum, Cologne

Italy:
Peggy Guggenheim Foundation, Venice

Spain:
Joan Miró Foundation, Barcelona
Maria Delors Miró Collection, Palma

Sweden
Nationalmuseum, Stockholm

United States:
Albright-Knox Art Gallery, Buffalo,
  New York
City Art Museum, St. Louis, Missouri
Cleveland Museum of Art, Cleveland
The Solomon R. Guggenheim Collection,
  New York
Museum of Modern Art, New York
Philadelphia Museum of Art, Pennsylvania

Glossary

Abstract art Paintings that consist entirely of patterns and shapes, and do not attempt to portray anything in the real world.

Avant-garde A phrase used to describe something that is ahead of its time.

Collage Building up a picture from pieces of colored material or paper.

Cubism An art movement, dating from 1907, in which paintings and sculptures were broken up into distorted shapes. The artists used muted colors and showed subjects from more than one angle.

Dada An art movement that included poetry, theater, and music as well as painting, and rejected traditional ways of creating art.

Fascism A political movement headed by a dictator that places the nation above the individual and forcibly suppresses opposition.

Fauvists This name was given to a loose-knit group of artists who painted in vivid colors in around 1905-8.

Lithographs Prints made from a stone print surface rather than a linoleum or metal one.

Nationalism Focusing on the interests of one's own country or area above all others.

Republicanism Favoring a form of government without a monarch.

Retrospective An exhibition, usually on a large scale, that looks back at the work of one particular artist over many years.

Surrealism An art movement (including poetry and theater) based on the exploration of dream worlds and the subconscious.

INDEX

INDEX OF PICTURES

PICTURE CREDITS:
Special thanks to Joan Miró Foundation, Barcelona; Joan Miro Foundation, Palma de Mallorca; Bridgeman Art Library; Frank Spooner Pictures; Design and Artists Copyright Society; ADAGP, Paris; The Estate of Joan Miró.